Donna Eichstaedt

SILVER CITY'S BEAR MOUNTAIN LODGE: THE UNTOLD STORY

DONNA EICHSTAEDT
2008

Silver City's Bear Mountain Lodge:
The Untold Story

ISBN #978-0-9822617-0-5 paper
Library of Congress

Editing: Dr. Carl Eichstaedt, Cheryl Fallstead
Technical: Gerald Rel
Cover photos: Courtesy of Bear Mountain Lodge
and the New Mexico Nature Conservancy
Lower Cover Photo by Alan Eckert

Southwest Senior Books
Las Cruces, New Mexico 88004
SWSenior.com

DEDICATION

I would like to dedicate this book to my 5 grandchildren, Gabriel, Cory, Carly, Jackson and Lanie. They enrich my life and inspire me to do great things about which they can be proud.

AUTHOR BIOGRAPHY

Donna March Eichstaedt is College Assistant Professor of History at Doña Community College in Las Cruces, New Mexico. Born in Peoria and raised in Normal, Illinois, she earned a doctorate in History at Illinois State University in 1990 and for the past 15 years has been teaching History—first for Troy State University at White Sands Missile Range, then at UTEP in El Paso, Texas, and now, at Doña Ana Community College. She taught and advised at Illinois State University and served as Dean of Lincoln College's Normal, Illinois extension campus for 13 years. Now living in Las Cruces, she has contributed feature articles for: *Southern New Mexico Destinations; Southern New Mexico Magazine* and *Southwest Senior newspaper.* She compiled and edited *Once Enemies, Now Friends* (Miles and Pfaeffle) in 2002 and writes regularly for *The Southern New Mexico Historical Review; Southwest Senior,* and numerous other publications. She is a board member of the Doña Ana County Historical Society and the Pan American Dance Institute of NMSU; studies flamenco dance; and along with her family, owns Red Sky Horse Farm in Las Cruces. She has been in Girl Scouting for 21 years and is presently a Girl Scout leader for her granddaughter's troop, also in Las Cruces. Besides having studied the history of New Mexico for the past 35 years, her special interest is in the History of WWII, Native American history and for 20 years, she has pursued Oral History interviews with veterans. She and her husband Carl travel extensively in Europe, following WWII Allied movements and talk to people about the war. They have two daughters, 5 grandchildren, 4 dogs, "too many" horses, and 4 very interesting and funny cats.

TABLE OF CONTENTS

LIST OF ILLUSTRATIONS

PREFACE

Deciding to write the history of a person or place generally begins with curiosity, and mine was definitely piqued one day in 1999 when, purely by chance, I drove down that long, narrow dirt road leading to the Bear Mountain Lodge just outside of Silver City, New Mexico. When I caught the first glimpse of the lodge, with its Spanish mission style architecture, nestled in that gorgeous valley between mountain ranges, I had a feeling it had a unique history. But when I walked up to the front door and read the note that said the owner, Mrs. Myra McCormick, was ill and the lodge was closed, I was even more intrigued. McCormick is a big name in American Gilded Age history. I wondered if she could be an heiress to the Cyrus McCormick reaper fortune, spending her life in a quaint and remote lodge in the wilderness of New Mexico. It wouldn't be unusual, as others from prominent families from the East have embraced the enchantment of New Mexico and spent their adult lives immersed in its history, art and culture—women like Mable Dodge Lujan and Millicent Rogers of Taos, for example.

Once I began to research the lodge and Mrs. McCormick, I learned that she was not from THE McCormick family, but rather a girl who grew up on a chicken farm in Pennsylvania. However, I was still curious, and once I met and interviewed the first owner, Juanita Franks of Silver City, and found out why the lodge was built, I knew this story needed to be told.

Myra McCormick died before I began research on the book, but the highlight of my quest was meeting the remarkable Juanita Franks, who was 97 on the day of my interview. She amazed me with her sharp memory, her sense of humor and most of all, her very positive attitude about her married life with Dr. Walter Langer, prominent 20th century psychoanalyst and partner in building the lodge. In spite of the tragedies and disappointments they shared in their early married life, and their eventual divorce, she expressed great admiration for him and seemed to harbor no regrets that uncontrollable historic circum- stances drove them apart, never to completely fulfill their original plan. That plan was to operate a school for emotionally disturbed boys in what is now the Bear Mountain Lodge.

There was no question in my mind that their story was compelling and would be of interest to people who are visiting the lodge or have stayed there. Walter Langer and Juanita Franks represented all that was good about their generation and all that was bad about the period of history they had to endure. The Bear Mountain Lodge stands as kind of a tribute to them, as well as to Mrs. McCormick's 40 years of hard work to keep it going. It is my hope that I can adequately tell the story—the untold story—of the interesting people who lived there, and of the building itself—a most significant New Mexico landmark.

Donna Eichstaedt

ACKNOWLEDGEMENTS

No one can research and write a book without the patience and encouragement of those around them. Therefore, I must say thank you to those people who have contributed the most to this book and to my peace of mind while writing it. First and foremost, I must thank my husband, Dr. Carl Eichstaedt, for his research help and critical editing. But most of all, I am grateful for his constant love and encouragement when my mind was elsewhere, and my body was glued to my computer. He has shared my love of New Mexico, its history, its people and its places, and has willingly accompanied me and taken part in research to the most distant of these.

Next, I must thank my lifelong friend Martha Gallo of Cape Cod, Massachusetts and Las Cruces, New Mexico, who has listened to my stories since we were eight or nine years old—and who is still listening!

I also want to thank my dear friend and former professor, Dr. Lawrence Walker, Professor of History Emeritus from Illinois State University, for his many years of encouragement in my academic career and most recently for the hundreds of emails of advice and ideas for whatever I write. He is a man of few words, but each that he offers is a gemstone.

There are also those whose incredible scholarly work has inspired me to keep researching and writing. They are Drs. John Freed and Mark Wyman, Professors Emeriti, Illinois State University. Their scholarly achievements are beyond remarkable.

There are others who have contributed significantly to this study. Linda Rowse of Silver City, New Mexico, shared endearing traits with me about her great-aunt, loaned me photos and personal correspondence, and enlightened me about parts of Juanita Frank's personality I would never have discovered. Shirley Franks, daughter of Juanita's brother Randolph and niece of Juanita's brother Alvin, sent precious photos of the Franks family and shared some pearls of information with me about them and the lodge. Randolph helped his mother run the ranch when she was widowed, and Alvin was actively involved in the operation of the lodge during the 1930's.

I am tremendously grateful to Dr. Sanford Gifford and archivist Olga Umansky at the Boston Psychoanalytic Society and Institute. They have enriched this study immensely by sharing with me valuable photos and documents pertaining to Walter Langer and the Freuds. They were gracious hosts during my research visit to the institute.

People from the New Mexico Nature Conservancy, the agency to whom the lodge was given by Mrs. McCormick, its previous owner, have been extremely helpful in sharing information, photos, and support. They are Terry Sullivan, Bob Findling and lodge general manager, Maura Monsior. I would be amiss if I did not thank the esteemed Dr. Dale Zimmerman for his most insightful information about Mrs. McCormick and the naturalist activities that went on at the lodge for 40 some years—not to mention his expertise in detailing the flora and fauna on the lodge property. My thanks also go to Harry Benjamin, Silver City artist; Joanne Woodward Cross, daughter of the lodge's builder; Jan Fallstead for her editing skills, and Lorraine Southward and Richard Majestic for computer assistance. I am also grateful to Keith Whelpley, who always trusts my writing and is willing to publish just about anything I submit! A special thanks goes to Gerald Rel, a long-time friend and the man who has lent artistic overlay and computer expertise to this book and to many of my writings in the past.

After visiting the newly remodeled Bear Mountain Lodge, I must also thank those people responsible for its beautiful "new image." Richard S. Bigelow of the Richard Bigelow Construction Co., Inc., was general contractor for the renovation of the lodge and was extremely helpful in providing details of the work done via many emails. He and the following businesses contributed to the remodeling of the lodge while retaining its historic charm. A big thanks to Santa Clara Woodworks, Gordon West; Pinos Altos Plumbing, Jeff Trinkle; Dement Electric, Rob & Beth Dement; Humble Enterprises, Kevin Humble; Donaldsen Drywall, Tex Donaldsen; Mountain Hues, Phil Thornton; and Greg Hartman, formerly of the FMSM Architectural Firm.

And last, but most certainly not least, I wish to give a special thanks to my new friend, Leonard Langer of Annisquam, Massachusetts, nephew of Walter Langer. Leonard graciously shared with me family documents of the remarkable Langer family and went out of his way to provide me with information and valuable photos.

Donna Eichstaedt
2008

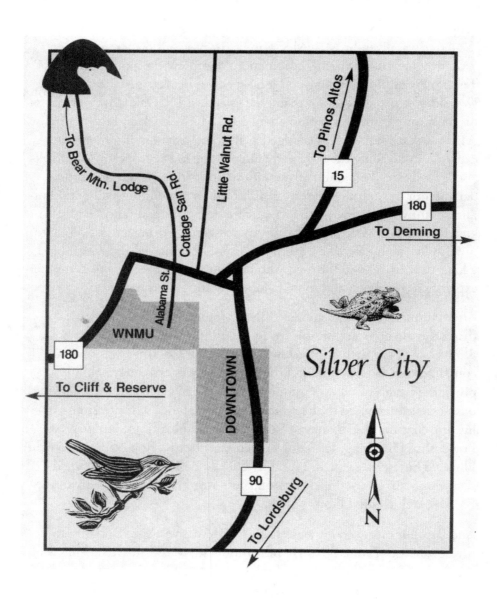

INTRODUCTION
New Mexico Territory 1910

In the early 1900s, immigrants from Europe were nourishing America's industry in the East, railroads stretched from coast to coast, and industrialization provided prosperity for some and modern conveniences for many. But in the West, life was still rough, rugged, and rural—and New Mexico territory was no exception. Mexicans were crossing the border to flee revolution and find work, gunfighters still squared off in the streets, and famed sheriff Pat Garrett was murdered in the desert outside Las Cruces in southern New Mexico.

Still very much a part of the Wild West, New Mexico became home to people who wanted to ranch, work on the railroad, or take a chance at mining. Despite the harsh conditions, they kept coming and many who ranched or farmed managed to live off the land. It was in this environment that Lillie and Samps Dye homesteaded 160 acres a few miles north of Silver City, New Mexico Territory, in 1910.[1]

Bear Mountain.

The Dye property was in the heart of cattle and mining country, nestled away in the Fleming range of the Pinos Altos Mountains and adjacent to the Gila National Forest. To the northwest lay Bear Mountain, with its towering 9,000 foot peaks, and to the east, the Santa Rita chain. Beyond the Santa Ritas lay the Black Range Mountains, and far to the south, Cook's Peak could be seen. Local lore says that a stage coach route traversed the property in the late 1800s, connecting Silver City to the mining town of Fleming.[2]

One can only speculate why the Dyes decided to relinquish the property, but in March of 1918, they sold out to Maggie and William C. Franks for the sum of only $10.[3] The Franks never lived on the property,

The Franks Family. Left to right: Randolph, Alvin, Lolabelle, Juanita & William.

but operated it as a ranch. William was able to secure a grazing permit to run cattle in the national forest, which was adjacent to his acreage. After his death in 1920 at the age of 47, Maggie continued ranching with the help of her son Randolph. She rode horses, drove cattle and managed to raise their children, two boys and two girls. One baby girl died at the age of three. To make ends meet, Maggie took in boarders and one of them was a 14-year-old boy who required special mental health care. His presence led to a visit by Walter Langer, a young Harvard psychology graduate. While in New Mexico, Langer met Maggie's daughter Juanita and a romance ensued. They were married in 1927 and in 1928, Maggie sold part of her ranch to the newlyweds. That same year, Walter and Juanita built on the property a school for disturbed young men, which today is the 80-year-old Bear Mountain Lodge in Silver City, now owned by the New Mexico Nature Conservancy and operated as a bed and breakfast.[4] It is with Juanita Franks and Walter Langer that the story of this remarkable place begins.

INTRODUCTION ENDNOTES

1. Myra McCormick, *Bear Mountain Ranch Recipes* (Tucson: Suhuaro Press, 1989), p. iii.

2. Harry G. Allen Jr., Bear Mountain Ranch brochure, 1937, p. 5 (Author's Library).

3. Miscellaneous Deed Records, Book K. 61, p. 491. Grant County, New Mexico.

4. Juanita Franks, Silver City, New Mexico, interview by Donna Eichstaedt, 1 August 2002.

CHAPTER I

The Beginning of a Legacy

Maggie Flurry Franks was a true New Mexico ranch woman of the early 20th century, having lived her entire life in a ranching family. After her marriage to William C. Franks in 1899, she and her husband farmed and ranched, first in Santa Rita and later a few miles west of Silver City. They ran cattle, mostly Herefords, under the brands WF, ZL, TY and the Flag.

Four children were born to William and Maggie, and all except one were delivered by their grandmother at home.[1] In a 1999 *Silver City Sun-News* article, her daughter Juanita explained: "My mother never went to a hospital one day in her life. Her philosophy was 'stay away from doctors and lawyers.'"[2]

After William passed away in 1920, Maggie began taking in boarders. The superintendent of schools knew Maggie, and began sending troubled young people to board with her. One of them was Pete Paine, an emotionally disturbed young man from a wealthy family in the East who had been sent to New Mexico by his doctor. The boy's uncle, a Frederick Winsor, paid the $200 monthly board bill. Maggie soon

Walter Langer

found her task too difficult, however, and it was decided the young man needed professional psychological help. As a result, Walter C. Langer, a young Harvard-trained psychologist, was hired by Mr. Winsor and sent to New Mexico to assist.[3]

Walter Langer had been working on his master's degree at Harvard with financial assistance from the government because of a World War I service-connected disability.

Walter Langer in WWI. Walter Langer the "Doughboy."

Pete Paine

With one year of eligibility left and deep into the study of Sigmund Freud and psychoanalysis, Langer was encouraged to undergo analysis himself. But with only a $100 per month stipend, he soon found it necessary to take on part-time teaching and other jobs. One of them was as a chauffeur for a wealthy family in Boston[4]. Even so, he was unable to meet his financial obligations and, in the spring of 1925 when he finally completed his master's degree, he was forced to discontinue analysis and prepare to go to work full-time. Complicating his financial situation were breathing difficulties caused by having been gassed on the battlefields of France in WWI. But soon the opportunity in New Mexico came his way:

My health throughout my college career had not been good, and I had to spend considerable time in the infirmary combating my respiratory difficulties. The Veteran's Administration doctors continually urged a change of climate, but I resisted on the grounds that I wanted to finish my academic career at Harvard before doing anything else. Besides, the country was still in a depression and jobs were not plentiful. Early in the summer of

Mr. & Mrs. Walter Langer

Maggie's brother, Alvin, Juanita and Walter circa 1928.

1925 fortune smiled upon me, when I was offered the opportunity of going out to New Mexico to check on an adolescent boy...who had been sent out there in the hope that he might make a better adjustment away from his family.[5]

The high, dry climate improved Langer's health, and he decided to stay on longer than intended. The boy also seemed to be improving and his family consented to continue the therapy for an indefinite period of time. As a result of this experience, Langer came to the important conclusion that treating mental illness when a person is young is more productive than waiting until adulthood. Furthermore, he believed that treatment would be most successful if these young patients were far removed from family, within which he believed were "constant pressures and conflicts...The result of my pondering was that I would make New Mexico, with its excellent climate, my permanent home and attempt to open a school there for adolescent neurotic boys."[6]

During Langer's stay in New Mexico, he and Maggie Franks' daughter Juanita, a school teacher, became acquainted and a romance blossomed. "So Walter came—we were all living with my mother and brother. And they liked him, and I saw him quite often. I liked him too."[7]

Eventually, Walter homesteaded in an abandoned cabin on some open land a few miles out of Silver City. Since Walter was a veteran, the government allowed him to live on the property and fix it up. After a year, he would be given a patent for the land.

This was the original plan, but in 1927 Walter and Juanita were married, and decided to build a school on the Franks' property. The $20,000 cost for the building was financed by Pete Paine's uncle, Frederick Winsor, who also suggested the Spanish Mission architectural style. Walter and Juanita's dream was about to became a reality.[8] Silver City carpenters, Clarence (Cal) and Walter Woodward erected the school (now the Bear Mountain Lodge), a laundry, two bedrooms and a garage.[9]

And so it was that Walter and Juanita Langer embarked on a new and experimental project, aimed at helping disturbed adolescent boys achieve a new start in life in the wilderness of New Mexico. Walter Langer's financial problems would soon be over—for a while at least—with the opening of The Rocky Mountain Ranch School.

A promotional brochure described it as, "a Mental Hygiene School for Boys On a ranch in the mountains of New Mexico."[10] The booklet was sent to psychiatrists and educators all over the country, and made it clear that the school was designed especially for "the pre-adolescent boy with psychopathic tendencies, unable to associate profitably with his comrades, unable to cope satisfactorily with his school work, suffering from a malignant emotional or mental disorder which prevents him from leading a happy, healthy, and useful life."[11]

The brochure listed distinguished professors and psychiatrists who would act as advisers to the school, and provide psychological expertise to "uncover the repressed longings, desire, and tendencies which are at work in his (the student's) unconscious mind."[12]

It also described the environment of the ranch school:

> The Rocky Mountain Ranch School, located 6000 feet above sea level, in the heart of the Sunshine State, in what is conceded to be one of the most healthful climates in the world, has unsurpassed facilities for building up the physical organism of the boy while developing him mentally. In this high, dry, cool, and invigorating region, where there are 360 days of sunshine yearly, it is possible to keep the boys out-of-doors the year round, under expert attendants. Each boy is provided with a cow-pony; riding, hiking, swimming, and all other forms of sport and play are carried on. The nature of the country with its odd geological formations, its fossils, mines, peculiar growth, and prehistoric Indian relics, as well as the modern atmosphere—the West, where big men do big things—furnishes

Rocky Mountain Ranch School under construction.

Proud owner, Walter Langer.

the boy with innumerable opportunities for sublimation (which) are found in no other locality.

> Being limited to an enrollment of eight boys, The Rocky Mountain Ranch School is able to maintain a true home atmosphere which is lacking in the larger institutions, and yet is essential to the emotional development of the child…. In short, The Rocky Mountain Ranch School has the facilities to give the abnormal boy exactly what he needs, mentally, physically, and educationally. [13]

Walter did the recruiting for the school—a job that took him to cities all over the United States and Canada. It must not have been easy, as transportation problems plagued him and he grew weary of living out of a suitcase. On one postcard sent to Juanita, his frustration is evident. "Could not make satisfactory arrangements on R.R. Started out and broke rear axle in a chuck hole 35 miles out of Cruces. Had to get towed in. Just arrived at 5:45. Tough luck. Love, Walter."[14] In another, he expresses joy at being in Alberta, Canada. "This is about the prettiest place I have ever seen."[15]

The school was quite successful. Langer was able to put all his psychological training to good use and Juanita, having received a bachelor's degree in home economics, served as housemother and teacher. "I was running the establishment…taking care of everything" she said in an interview in 2002.[16]

Langer was soon able to repay his debt to Dr. Martin Peck, from whom he had received psychoanalysis back in Boston earlier in the decade. But the Langer's prosperity didn't last long, as the stock market crashed in 1929, resulting in several students leaving the school. Most were from well-to-do families in the East who could not continue to bear the cost of their sons' specialized education in such a distant place. Several parents encouraged the Langers to bring the school and the concept to Boston, and if so, they would continue their sons' education there.[17] As the Depression deepened, the Langers opted to do just that. In an interview in 2002, Juanita recalled those difficult days at the school, "I think there were seven or eight kids towards the end there when the crash came in '29, and our income ceased pretty fast. So shortly after that we decided, well, maybe we ought to go East instead and see if we could do better back there. I thought that's what he would like to do, and I was agreeable."[18]

And so it was, in 1930, they moved to Boston and started over—far from the solitude of New Mexico. Walter had been born and raised in Boston, so the move may have been easy for him. But for Juanita, such a change proved challenging for a ranch girl from the Southwest.

Front entrance.

East side.

The Great Room eastside.

The Great Room westside.

School's year round sleeping porch.

Horseback riding at Rocky Mountain Ranch School.

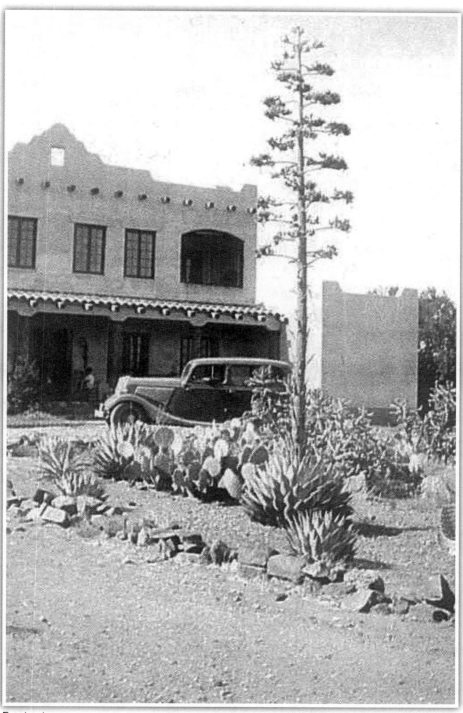

Front entrance.

CHAPTER I ENDNOTES

1. Charles Coan, "Mrs. Maggie Flurry Franks," *The American Historical Review* 32 (April 1927): 366-67.

2. "Juanita Franks: "So Much to Tell you." *Silver City Sun-News*, 1 November 1999.

3. Juanita Franks, Silver City, New Mexico. Interview by Sanford Gifford, Boston Psychoanalytic Society and Institute, 22 May 1999. (Transcript, p. 2). (Author's Library).

4. Walter Langer, letter to William Langer, 22 August 1974. (Author's Library).

5. Walter C. Langer and Sanford Gifford, "An American Analyst in Vienna during the Anschluss," *Journal of the History of the Behavioral Sciences* XIV (January 1978):48.

6. Langer and Gifford.

7. Gifford interview with Juanita Franks. (Transcript, p. 3).

8. Gifford interview with Juanita Franks. (Transcript, pp. 3-4).

9. Joanne Woodward Cross, Silver City, New Mexico. Interview by Donna Eichstaedt, 2 November 2007.

10. Walter C. Langer, "The Rocky Mountain Ranch School" brochure, n.d. (Author's Library).

11. The Rocky Mountain Ranch School brochure.

12. The Rocky Mountain Ranch School brochure.

13. The Rocky Mountain Ranch School brochure.

14. Walter C . Langer, letter to Juanita Franks Langer, 1928. (Author's Library).

15. Walter C. Langer, postcard to Juanita Franks Langer, n.d. (Author's Library).

16. Eichstaedt interview with Juanita Franks.

17. Gifford interview with Juanita Franks. (Transcript p. 4).

18. Gifford interview with Juanita Franks. (Transcript p. 4).

CHAPTER II

Juanita and Walter's Early Years: Joy and Sorrow

Juanita Franks and Walter Langer grew up in two distinct and different environments. Juanita's grandparents were immigrants from Switzerland who had come to the United States after the Civil War and pioneered in New Mexico. She was born in New Mexico territory in 1903, in the little mining town of Ivanhoe and first attended school in Pinos Altos, New Mexico. Like many rural American children of the early 20th century, she rode a horse to school and was taught in one room with children of all ages who drank water from a bucket and were warmed by a wood stove. "We never had a toothbrush," she said, "but we ate a lot of apples."[1] Eventually, she moved with her parents, two brothers and a sister to Silver City where the family lived in what she described as "a beautiful house because it had a bath tub, toilet and sink."[2]

In 1926, in the middle of the Roaring '20s, Juanita graduated from New Mexico Teachers College in Silver City (now Western New Mexico University) with a degree in home economics education. She taught school in and around the Silver City area for a couple of years until she married Walter Langer. Together they tried to offer a unique and much-needed school for disturbed adolescent boys on ranch land adjacent to the Gila National Forest, but with its closing in 1929, Juanita's life would take a turn that would send her away from New Mexico—the only place she had ever known, and into the big city of Boston.[3]

Walter, on the other hand, was the third son of German immigrants who came to the U.S. in the closing years of the 19th century and settled in a lower-middle class

COURTESY OF LEONARD LANGER

Walter on the left; Rudolph in the middle; William on the right, Mrs. Langer, forefront.

Irish-German neighborhood in Boston. Walter never knew his father, who died before he was born. Although his father had achieved moderate financial success with a flower shop, upon his death Mrs. Langer had to work in dressmaking and take in boarders. In his autobiography, William Langer called his brother "a child of sorrow" because of having no father and two older brothers who, he admitted, often excluded him.

Walter graduated from Rindge Technical School in Cambridge, and originally planned to become an electrician. But, after a short stint in that field, he decided to head in another direction. He later passed the entrance exams for Harvard, but WWI intervened, and he soon found himself in the trenches of France.

The Pulsifer Estate in Auburndale, Massachusetts

After being gassed (one of the most debilitating injuries suffered by our troops in the first World War), Walter was deemed 56% disabled. As a result, he received a government stipend of $100 per month, which paid for his tuition at Harvard once the war was over. His experiences in the trenches provided the impetus to study human behavior and the stipend allowed him to follow his interests and major in psychology.[5]

It was because of this training that Walter Langer found himself in New Mexico, and with the help of his new wife, Juanita, would create a school for psychotic boys that would be the first of its kind. In spite of the setback they suffered when the Depression forced parents to pull their children from the school, Juanita and Walter forged on and started over in Boston.

For Walter, the move to the East Coast brought him back to the city where he was born, raised and schooled. His mother, two brothers and Harvard professors were all there. He had connections and made the transition smoothly. For Juanita, it wasn't so easy. "I didn't like it," she said. "I had one cold after another and sometimes you'd go as long as 30 days and never see the sun."[6]

Once back home, Walter was able to negotiate the purchase of the Pulsifer Estate on Islington Road in Auburndale, Massachusetts. The Moorish style mansion constructed of granite stone was formerly a Boston landmark, the Castle Inn Hotel, which sat on a peninsula that jutted out into the Charles River. Walter felt he had made the right choice of location for the school. "It was a gorgeous spot and ideal for my purpose, since we had plenty of room and no close neighbors."[7]

In spite of Juanita's discomfort in the East, she made the best of it. She remembered that the estate was huge. "I've forgotten how many rooms, and a stable and barn out back, and servants' quarters and all kinds of things....Well, it was a building that was built after something in England, so I was told."[8] Juanita also remembered that when she told her mother how big the estate was, Maggie, who raised turkeys in New Mexico, shipped her daughter five half-grown birds.[9]

Boston Globe.

Some remodeling and redecorating needed to be done to the building before it could be transformed into a school, but the prospects looked bright. Walter named it The Langer School for Boys and by September several new students had enrolled, in addition to some who had been with the Langers in New Mexico. But fate dealt them a blow on one freezing night in December 1931, when the building caught fire and burned to the ground.[10] In a letter to Dr. Sanford Gifford of the Boston Psychoanalytic Society in 1975, Walter stated the cause of the fire to be defective wiring.[11] In his autobiography, William Langer noted that the fire could not be contained because the hydrants were frozen.[12] However, a Boston Globe newspaper article the next day told of hydrants far removed from the scene, as well as water from the nearby Charles River, being utilized. Firefighters answering the call from three nearby towns found the school completely engulfed in flames, but continued to spray in spite of collapsing walls. The deep cold was also cited as a problem as water from the hoses rapidly turned the grounds around the building into a sheet of ice. Furthermore, the clothes of the firefighters were crusted with ice and fire hoses were frozen to the

19

ground. The four instructors and three students living at the school were roused from their sleep by Langer, who braved smoke-filled hallways to sound the alarm.[13]

The school was so totally destroyed that little was left standing except two pillars. Leonard Langer, Walter's nephew, remembers having gone the next day to see the ruins of his uncle's school for boys. "I have a clear memory during my first visit of the massive billiard table on the second floor, which together with a grand piano came crashing down through the floors and ending up in the basement ruins."[14]

With no insurance and the cost of redecorating having been paid for with credit, the Langers were forced into bankruptcy. Walter Langer was devastated: "It not only destroyed the school but me along with it."[15]

Fate dealt the Langers another blow when a chimney fire damaged the school they had left behind in New Mexico. Juanita returned to Silver City alone and with help from her brother Alvin, turned the school she and Langer had built into her home. She never returned to Boston. With plans dashed and living apart from Juanita, Walter suffered alone in Boston, as letters to his wife reveal. In a letter written in October of 1934, Walter, who had returned to Harvard, congratulated Juanita on securing a job as a social service consultant, but lamented his precarious financial and educational situation:

> I was happy to get your letter containing all the good news. I am glad to hear that good fortune is smiling on others even though it has not yet begun to shine on me....I did not manage to finish up my doctorate in the Spring but hope to do so at mid-year this year....It has been very hard for me to get along at all for jobs are still very scarce and I have been forced to do all sorts of work at very low rates to keep going at all.[16]

Life in Boston continued to be difficult for Walter and a lack of finances prohibited him from visiting Juanita in New Mexico. In the same letter he expresses a desire to return to New Mexico. "I often think of the old place and the mountains. I certainly wish that it was possible for me to get out there sometime for a vacation to go fishing, hunting, or what not. I certainly do miss that country and there is no place I would sooner go to spend a vacation."[17]

It was not to be. Juanita noted in an interview that she attended a social work meeting in Atlantic City, New Jersey, in 1936 and he joined her there. "And that's the last time I saw him."[18] They were amicably divorced that same year.

Each pursued individual interests, and both became prominent in two different worlds: Walter as an eminent psychoanalyst and the foremost expert on Adolf Hitler and Juanita as the owner of Bear Mountain Lodge, which became her home and later a country club and hotel. A local newspaper described the conversion:

> Mrs. Walter Langer is converting her spacious and beautiful home, located four miles north of Silver City, off the Cottage Sanatorium Road, into a country club and hotel, which she has named the Bear Mountain Lodge. The site is one of the most beautiful for the purpose of this section. It is a 10 minute ride by automobile from the city…The house contains eight guest rooms, and large sleeping porches. It is electrically lighted and has a large electrical system. Saddle horses can be secured there and riding in the Gila National Forest will afford patrons a rare pleasure from a scenic and every other standpoint.[19]

With the help of her brother Alvin, who built a five-hole, nine-tee golf course at the club, she put in a swimming pool, offered horseback riding and became well known for her Sunday evening fried chicken dinners. The Tulloch family of Silver City often told of the many times they delivered a hundred dressed chickens for a dinner at the club.[20] A local newspaper described the new golf course in detail:

Remnants of 1930's swimming pool.

> One of the newest features added to the lodge is the construction of a five-hole golf course with

the first tee directly in front of the house. The course is undergoing final construction this week with Alvin Franks, brother of Mrs. Langer, in charge. It was laid out by Carl Frymire and is said to be one of the sportiest in this section. Two of the holes are located in an unusually appealing position. One shot is over a mountain, dropping down into a wide clearing. The other is from the top of a high hill, the distance of which is 170 yards.[21]

In another newspaper article, it was noted that Bear Mountain Lodge was quite modern, with "steam heat and running hot and cold water, four bathrooms with showers, telephone and electric lights. "[22]

Walter, having finally completed his doctorate in psychology from Harvard in 1935, joined the faculty at Columbia Teachers' College. While there, he became a staff member of the Progressive Education Association, which was being sponsored by the Rockefeller Foundation. Through that association, he was asked to write a psychology textbook for high school seniors and college freshman. The outcome was *Psychology and Human Living*, the proceeds from which were enough to send him to Vienna for two years to fulfill his dream of being psychoanalyzed by Sigmund Freud's daughter, Anna, and to study at the Vienna Psychoanalytic Institute.[23]

Back in New Mexico, times were tough and in 1934 Juanita decided to return to school to pursue a master's degree at the Denver School of Social Work. Though she did not graduate, Juanita was offered a job in Denver and stayed there a year. After that she returned to Silver City and worked for the county in the field of social work. When the Emergency Relief Organization was set up under Roosevelt's New Deal program, she got a job traveling all over the state of New Mexico, doing food planning for diabetics and people who were out of work.[24] In 1936*, Juanita sold the lodge and remained in the field of social work for the rest of her life.[25] Many owners followed, but none would be as prominent as Juanita Franks and Walter Langer.

*A brochure distributed by Harry Allen Jr. dated 1937 suggests that Juanita may have leased the ranch for a year or two before selling it to Mr. and Mrs. Horton in 1938.

There is no record of a sale in 1936 to Harry Allen Jr. in Grant County, New Mexico, deed books.

The Ranch House.

BEAR MOUNTAIN RANCH

SILVER CITY
NEW MEXICO

Eastern Representative
JOHN H. ALLEN
2401 Daily News Bldg.
220 E. 42nd St.
New York
Murray Hill 2-7398

Operated by
HARRY G. ALLEN, JR.
Mail Address: P. O. Box 191,
Silver City, New Mex.

23

CHAPTER II ENDNOTES

1. *Silver City Sun-News*, 1 November, 1999.

2. *Silver City Sun-News*, 1 November, 1999.

3. Eichstaedt interview with Juanita Franks.

4. William Langer, *The Illustrious Langers: In and Out of the Ivory Tower*, (New York: Neale Watson Academic Publishing Company, 1977), p. 22.

5. Walter Langer, letter to William Langer, p. 5

6. Eichstaedt interview with Juanita Franks.

7. Langer and Gifford, p. 49.

8. Gifford interview with Juanita Franks. (Transcript, p. 4).

9. Gifford interview with Juanita Franks. (Transcript, p. 5).

10. *Boston Globe*, 9 December 1931.

11. Walter Langer, letter to Sanford Gifford, Boston Psychoanalytic Society and Institute Archives. Walter Langer papers, 1935-2001, MS. N-007. 11 November 1975.

12 William Langer, *The Illustrious Langers: In and Out of the Ivory Tower*, p. 166.

13. *Boston Globe*, 9 December 1931.

14. Leonard Langer, email to Donna Eichstaedt, 9 September 2007. (Author's Library)

15. Langer and Gifford, p. 49.

16. Walter C. Langer, letter to Juanita Franks Langer, 12 October 1934, p. 1 (Author's Library).

17. Walter C. Langer, letter to Juanita Franks Langer.

18. Gifford interview, (Transcript, p. 5).

19. *Silver City Independent*,14 June, 1932.

20. Myra McCormick, *Bear Mountain Ranch Recipes*, p. iv.

21. *Silver City Independent*,14 June 1932.

22. *Silver City Enterprise*, 17 June 1932.

23. Walter C. Langer, letter to William Langer, p. 5.

24. Gifford interview, (Transcript, p. 5).

25. McCormick, p. iv.

CHAPTER III

Juanita and Walter on the International Scene: 1936-1945

Having sold Bear Mountain Lodge and wanting to do something for the war effort, Juanita signed up as a volunteer in a Red Cross medical unit. Her social work training was put to good use when she was sent to hospitals in England, Scotland, Wales and France. "When they fitted us out with clothes and I got warm ones, I knew I'd be going someplace cold."[1] She recalled that during the week of D-Day, June 6-12, 1944, one thousand soldiers were cared for each day at the hospital to which she was assigned. There were also many occasions to take cover in shelters from the V-1 and V-2 rockets that fell on England during the war.[2] Juanita served in France as well, as a photograph showing her in uniform with five other Red Cross volunteers is inscribed, "Juanita, fourth from the left, in France on her way to the Battle of the Bulge."[3] (General Eisenhower insisted that all civilians traveling with the military be in uniform.)

COURTESY OF SHIRLEY AND ALVIN FRANKS

WWII Red Cross Social workers, Juanita 2nd from Right.

After the war, Juanita returned to New Mexico and went to work at the Veterans' Hospital at Fort Bayard, just outside of Silver City. While there, Juanita was responsible for integrating the wards at the hospital. She stated in an interview that one of the first things she did upon her arrival at the fort was to suggest to the doctors that patients be hospitalized in appropriate wards depending upon their infirmity rather than their race. At Fort Bayard, black patients were hospitalized together on one floor without consideration for their illness or injury. In spite of opposition by some of the doctors, the changes were made and the transition was smooth. When interviewed in 2002, Juanita noted, "I am very happy I made that suggestion."[4]

Juanita Franks remained in New Mexico the rest of her life. Along with a career in social work, she managed the family's vast ranch holdings, developed large sections of it, sold real estate, and still made time to raise

Juanita Franks riding a horse on her 100th birthday

Miss Me – But Let Me Go

When I come to the end of the road
and the sun has set for me
I want no rites in a gloom filled room!
Why cry for a soul set free!
Miss me a little-but not too long
and not with your head bowed low!
Remember the love that we once shared
Miss me – But let me go!
For this is a journey we all must take
and each must go alone;
it's all a part of the Master's plan
a step on the road home
when you are lonely and sick at heart
go to the friends we know
and bury your sorrows in doing good deeds
Miss me – But let me go.

In Loving Memory

JUANITA FRANKS

Born
Tuesday January 20, 1903 Ivanhoe, New Mexico

Passed Away
Thursday March 9, 2006 Silver City, New Mexico

Memorial Services Held At
Bright Funeral Home
Saturday March 11, 2006
2:00 PM

Conducted By
Mr. Floyd Robertson
Mr. Mike Rowse

Arrangements By
BRIGHT FUNERAL HOME
Silver City, NM

Juanita Frank's funeral memorial

a niece and nephew. Linda Rowse of Silver City remembers being a troubled teenager and going to live with her great-aunt Juanita. "She raised my brother and me from our teen years through adulthood."[5] Linda also told of Juanita's kindness in taking in strangers if they needed a place to stay, and she knows many people Juanita rescued from homelessness and abusive relationships. Juanita sheltered many Mexican nationals seeking work in the U.S., and was "written up" many times by the Border Patrol. They supposedly told her that if she kept it up, they'd put her in jail, but she never stopped. The desire to help others remained strong within Juanita Franks her entire life. She possessed an open mind, was liberal in her thinking, and had a zest for adventure that never waned. At the age of 100, she rode a horse, and on her 103rd birthday, her family took her swimming.[6]

Juanita Franks lived through historic times, made the best of life's challenges, and left a lasting impression on those who knew and would long remember her. She died in 2006 at the age of 103 in Silver City.[7] It was the only place she ever really wanted to be.

As for Walter Langer, his life was filled with adventure as well. His dream of traveling to Vienna and being psychoanalyzed by Anna Freud came true in 1936, but once there, storm clouds of an impending war began to hang over the city. Germany was flexing her muscles and it looked as though Austria would be her next victim. Nonetheless, he began his psychoanalysis with Anna Freud and studies at the Vienna Psychoanalytic Institute. His analysis sessions with Anna were held at the Freud summer home in Grinzing, on the outskirts of the city and Walter enjoyed daily morning visits with Professor Freud in the garden.

While their work continued, the political climate was becoming even more ominous. "Work at the Institute continued unabated and I believe that most of us tried to ignore the course of events, in the hope that they had reached their limit and that somehow we would be spared. But it was not to be."[8]

In March of 1938, Germany annexed Austria, in what is known as the "Anschluss." In an autobiographical article written in 1978, Walter remembered the day the Nazis marched into Vienna:

> I remember standing on the Ringstrasse as the Nazi war machine moved in to occupy the country. It was a sad moment, particularly when the populace that lined the streets gazed at this show of might in total silence, for a time, and then, here

Sigmund Freud and his dog in the garden in Vienna, Circa 1936-1938.

Anna Freud in Vienna, Circa 1936-1938.

and there, a voice would shout "Heil Hitler." Gradually the frequency increased until quite suddenly, as though awakened from a dream, everybody seemed determined to out-shout his neighbor and out-reach him in giving the Nazi salute.[9]

Discrimination against Jews and roundups of Vienna's intellectual community, anti-Nazis, and others who Hitler deemed dangerous, soon began. Psychoanalysts were particularly targeted since many were Jewish. Every day more and more were arrested and shipped off by the truckloads to concentration camps. Fear was everywhere. "Everybody kept quiet and tried to look the other way. Nobody trusted anybody else and it was dangerous to talk on the telephone, let alone in the coffee houses as we were accustomed to do."[10]

The publication wing of the Vienna Psychoanalytic Institute was confiscated and the Freud house searched. Even so, Walter was able to continue his personal analysis with Anna, though she was called in for questioning several times

Vienna Psychoanalytic Institute under Nazi control

Same building – Sigmund Freud Museum today

by the Gestapo. Acquaintances of Walter's, mostly those involved with the Institute, began to ask him for help in leaving the country. On several occasions, he housed a few in his apartment and even assisted in numerous clandestine escapes. He and a friend who had a car were able to drive those wishing to leave to the Italian or French borders, but in time Nazi border patrols tightened their grip.

Realizing that smuggling friends across borders was too hazardous, Walter decided to seek sponsors in the United States for people needing to leave Austria. With affidavits of support, it would be easier to leave Austria and be admitted to the United States as political refugees. He began the project by traveling back to the United States and asking fellow analysts in New York and Boston to sign affidavits of support that could be taken back to Vienna to be used by those in danger.[11]

After consulting with friends about his plan, Walter traveled to Cherbourg, France, and boarded the Queen Mary for the U.S. After a week of seeking affidavits in Boston and New York, he returned on the Normandie to France, and by train to Vienna. Most people he contacted in the United States were eager to help, though there were some who could have contributed much more, but who chose to sign only one affidavit or

31

none.[12] The person with the most modest income offered to sign several affidavits, saying: "Hell, Walter...I was born in Vienna and I could be any one of the thousands of people you describe. What do you want me to sign and how many?"[13] Walter pointed out to him that he might have to support some of these people after they reached the United States, to which he said: "I'll share my last piece of bread with any of them if we can only get them out."[14] Among the people who agreed to sponsor refugees was Felix Frankfurter, a native of Vienna, Austria, and soon to be a justice of the Supreme Court under President Franklin Delano Roosevelt.[15]

Walter returned the following week to Vienna with 50 affidavits, but noticed that conditions had worsened considerably during his absence and he was besieged with requests for help in getting out of the city. He managed to take care of other analysts first and then distributed the remaining affidavits to teachers, doctors, physicists, engineers, chemists, artists, and anthropologists. He later learned that all of those he was able to help succeeded in establishing themselves in the United States and not a single sponsor was ever asked to contribute a dollar to their support.

Walter's next concern was for Dr. Freud and his daughter Anna. Freud had consistently stated he did not want to leave Vienna in spite of Nazi occupation, but with deteriorating conditions and more and more pressure from friends, the professor agreed to go. What followed were lengthy negotiations between the Freuds and the Nazis, with the final outcome being that the family was given a permit to leave. But this did not necessarily guarantee escape from the country as the Gestapo had stepped up harassment at the border. As a result, Langer volunteered to accompany the Freuds on their train trip to France and on to London, where the professor had been invited to live. Professor Freud gratefully accepted Walter's offer.[16]

Walter arranged to take the same train as the Freuds and secured a compartment near theirs:

> Everything went smoothly until we reached the German-French border late at night. As the Nazi officials entered and examined one compartment after another, I could often hear altercations and a few persons were taken from the train for further examination. I took up a position directly in front of the compartments occupied by the Freuds and after an eternity the Nazi party arrived. They asked me what I was doing

there at that hour of night and I told them they were making so damn much noise that I could not sleep. They entered the Freud compartments and as I could determine they were reasonably polite and everything went off smoothly.[17]

Langer had successfully distracted the Nazi boarding party, and soon the train was on its way again. Perhaps the Nazi officials did not want to make a scene with an American since we were not yet at war with Germany. It must surely have been stressful for Walter and the Freuds. Walter recalled the moment when they knew all was well, "Searching the entire train required a considerable amount of time and it was not until the train crossed the river into France that we were able to breathe freely and drop off to sleep."[18]

Letters to Walter from Anna Freud in the 1970s confirm her admiration for what he did in Vienna and recall the fear that gripped her in those harrowing days:

> Reading your account of the Hitler time gave me many details of which I knew nothing at the time. Of course I remember your trip to America and your return with the affidavits. What I had not known was that there were 50 of them, almost unbelievable…I had not known of the trips to the border which you describe. It brought back the difficulties and hazards of the time and the many heartbreaking stories one had to listen to. What I remember most vividly myself were the nights when one inevitably expected the Nazi search parties to arrive. [19]

Walter made one more clandestine trip back to Vienna to rescue an old friend, but the Gestapo, by now apparently suspicious of his meanderings, paid a visit to his hotel room and ordered him to leave the next day. He was informed that his friend had been arrested, tried, and found guilty of crimes against the Third Reich and was no longer in Vienna. Walter walked the streets in the Ringstrasse that night, but became depressed at what he saw as a "lifeless" city. He wrote, "The monotony of the 'Heil Hitler' greetings that one encountered on every turn pounded in my ears like a death knell. I retreated to my hotel room and packed my things. The next morning I was on the plane for London, never to see Vienna (or his friend) again." [20]

After a stay of several months in London, associating with other

Langer's book on Hitler

Langer in retirement in Florida

analysts and the Freud circle of friends, Walter ran out of money and returned to the United States. A personal warm farewell and a sincere thank you from Professor Freud sent Walter back to Boston feeling as though his efforts had been worthwhile. "I was never so deeply touched as when he said goodbye and looked into my eyes with an expression I have never seen before or since."[21] A few months later Sigmund Freud was dead.

Upon returning to the United States in late 1938, Walter set up practice as an analyst in New York City. He soon found out, however, that he was not welcome when he attempted to join the New York Psychoanalytic Society and Institute. The reason for the cold shoulder was due to the fact that non-medical psychoanalysts were not readily accepted in the United States, as they were in Vienna. Walter was a Ph.D., not a medical doctor. It also became clear that New York City's weather made his breathing problems worse, so he returned to Cambridge where he set up his practice near Harvard University. At first, he faced discrimination from the Boston-area psychoanalytic community for the same reason he was shunned in New York, but he finally gained acceptance and became the first non-medical doctor accepted into society membership.[22]

When the United States entered WWII, Walter was recruited to spend three days each week in Washington, D.C., working on psychological warfare and problems of domestic morale for the Office of Strategic Services (the precursor to the CIA). In time, he was asked to work on

Freud's photo inscribed to Walter

a research project regarding the psychological state of Adolf Hitler. It was because of this study, "Analysis of the Personality of Adolph Hitler," that Walter soon gained international prominence. In it, he predicted Hitler's suicide toward the end of the war should Germany begin to lose.[23] The study was classified until 1971 and shortly thereafter, published in book form as *The Secret Wartime Report: The Mind of Adolf Hitler* [24] It still stands as the definitive study of Adolf Hitler.

Walter continued to work as an analyst in the Boston area after the war, but eventually moved to the Annisquam area outside the city and dabbled in real estate. However, his health continued to deteriorate and he knew another life change would have to occur, "The New England summers were fine but the winters were taking a heavy toll and if it had not been for the greenhouse to whose balmy climate I would retreat over weekends, I don't think I would have lasted as long as I did." [25]

In 1961 he retired to Sarasota, Florida, where he resided until his death in 1987.[26]

CHAPTER III ENDNOTES

1. *Silver City Sun-News*, 1 November 1999.

2. Eichstaedt interview with Juanita Franks.

3. Shirley Franks to Donna Eichstaedt, 15 September 2007. (Author's Library)

4. *Silver City Sun-News*, 1 November 1999.

5. Linda Rowse, Silver City, New Mexico, Interview by Donna Eichstaedt, 24 August 2007.

6. Linda Rowse interview.

7. *Silver City Daily Press*, 10 March 2006.

8. Langer and Gifford, p. 43.

9. Langer and Gifford, p. 39.

10. Langer and Gifford.

11. Langer and Gifford, pp. 43-44.

12. Langer and Gifford, p. 44.

13. Langer and Gifford.

14. Langer and Gifford.

15. Langer and Gifford.

16. Langer and Gifford.

17. Anna Freud, letter to Walter Langer, Boston Psychoanalytic Society and Institute Archives. Walter Langer papers, 1935-2001, MS.N-007, 19 July 1978.

18. Langer and Gifford, p. 46.

19. Langer and Gifford.

20. Walter Langer, letter to Sanford Gifford, Boston Psychoanalytic Society and Institute Archives, Walter C. Langer papers, 1972-1981, MS. N-007, 11 November 1972.

21. Langer and Gifford, p. 46.

22. Langer and Gifford.

23. U.S., Office of Strategic Services, Reports of the U.S. Government. "Analysis of the Personality of Adolph Hitler,"1943. http://www.lawschool.cornell.edu/library/donovan/Hitler/>.

24. Walter C. Langer. *The Mind of Adolf Hitler: The Secret Wartime Report*, New York: Basic Books, Inc., 1972.

25. Walter C. Langer, letter to William Langer, pp. 6-7. (Author's Library)

26. Obituary, Boston Psychoanalytic Society and Institute Archives Website, 17 July 2007, < HYPERLINK "http://www.bostonpsychoanalytic.org/library" http://www.bostonpsychoanalytic.org/library>

CHAPTER IV

Bear Mountain Ranch: New Owners – New Purposes

In the years following the Franks-Langer ownership, the lodge changed hands several times. There were occasional tourists, but more popular still was the use of the lodge's great room or patio for weddings and receptions. Juanita sold the lodge in 1936 and a fairly elaborate 1937 brochure listed Harry C. Allen Jr. as proprietor. The brochure promoted the lodge as the Bear Mountain Ranch and pointed out that horseback riding was the major attraction:

> We maintain a string of carefully selected horses. Upon arrival, each guest is assigned his own horse and saddle…Special instruction will gladly be given to guests who are inexperienced riders…All-day horseback trips into the Gila National Forest, with a pack mule or two, to carry provisions, are not infrequent. Moonlight rides in the mountains, campfires high up on the range, the old cowboy songs and stories—these will warm your heart to Bear Mountain and the southwest.[1]

Hunting was also emphasized in the brochure, with the ranch offering fully outfitted pack trips deep into the wilderness for fishing, hunting or camping. Opportunities for big game hunting are also mentioned and one photo in the brochure shows a fairly large, recently killed black bear strung up from a tree limb while another shows numerous deer ready to be dressed out. Though stating that the ranch is not a cattle operation, the brochure does offer opportunities for guests to participate in cattle round-ups and brandings at neighboring ranches. Other photos show guests on horseback fording a river during a pack trip, fishing in pristine mountain streams and attending rodeos.[2]

Harry Allen, Jr.

In 1938, a Mr. and Mrs. Horton and their son Bob purchased the property to operate it as a dude ranch. According to a newspaper advertisement, Bear Mountain Ranch offered the solitude that "makes for recreation and relaxation amid unexcelled conveniences for comfort and undisturbed enjoyment off the beaten path of congested tourist highways."[3] The ad also described the ranch's pristine location:

> Open all year round to guests—the ranch is five miles from Silver City nestled in the shadow of majestic Bear Mountain of the Pinos Altos Range, gateway to the Gila National Forest and Gila Cliff Dwellings, with a famous panorama covering a 50-mile sweep to the south and east. Located in a setting of natural beauty of unspoiled scenic wonderland, yet accessible to the last frontier of the West's bonanza mining region and its most colorful and historic cowtowns, whose hospitality is renowned.[4]

It also touted recent improvements and emphasized that, "For Your Vacation, Bear Mountain Ranch is the Ideal Rendezvous in the vast open spaces of the Southwest."[5]

The Hortons attracted guests from all over the U.S., as well as distant places like Panama, South Africa and China.[6] During World War II, airmen from a base in nearby Deming frequented the ranch. When Mr. Horton was killed in a one-car auto accident in Silver City, Mrs. Horton moved to Albuquerque, where she lived until her death in the early 1990s.[7] In May of 1946, George and Anna Kinsinger and Anna's sister, Mrs. Charles Townsend of Lakewood, Colorado, purchased the ranch for $40,000 for the purpose of operating it as a convalescent home. Renaming it Bear Mountain Rest Home, they advertised it as "one of the most beautiful mountain settings in the Southwest."[8]

The Kinsingers made it known that their facilities were ideal "for people seeking a place to recuperate from illness or operation...or

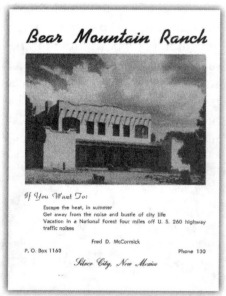

Bear Mountain Ranch under McCormick ownership: Notice change of roof facade from Chapter I. ranch photos.

those just desiring rest."[9] Yet another source indicates that the Kinsingers and their two daughters bought the ranch and opened it to the public. Their advertising brochure promoted, "Fun in Sunland! Such Variety of Scenery! So Many Ways to Enjoy it! A Friendly Home for it All!" Calling it Bear Mountain Ranch, it emphasized great weather, real Western hospitality, and wholesome recreation for the whole family.[10] They continued the ranch atmosphere that had existed with earlier owners, but at the same time stressed that their establishment was not a guest or dude ranch—but rather a "country home, western in atmosphere, hospitable, comfortable, and with home cooking and wholesome family surroundings."[11]

It was also during the Kinsinger years that the cast of the locally filmed classic movie, "The Salt of the Earth," stayed at the ranch. Will Geer, the grandpa on "The Waltons" TV series was among them.[12] In 1954, the local newspaper reported that the Kinsingers sold the ranch for $10,000, far below their purchase price, to a couple from Grand Rapids, Michigan, Clayton and Emma Zaagman.[13] A different source indicated that the Zaagmans bought the ranch at a judicial sale on a mortgage foreclosure. Silver City attorney J.R. Winkle bid on the property for $24,000 as a representative of Mr. Zaagman, who was described as the owner of the first mortgage on the property. Furthermore, it listed George Kinsinger as previous owner and defendant in the case, along with Mrs. Inez Horton, who held the second mortgage.[14]

The Zaagmans did not operate the lodge, but rather leased it in the mid-1950s to a Duke and Duchess D'Autry. The Duke and Duchess, it was reported, had moved to Silver City from Pecos County, Texas, where the Duke had been involved in uranium deals. Silver City's elite welcomed them with open arms. The woman who worked for the Duke as a secretary later told of the D'Autry's elegant lifestyle. She described a bed made out of teakwood and an upstairs bed coverlet made of mink. While working there, she also noticed many boxes full of art objects. The D'Autrys didn't stay long, however, as it became obvious they had left Texas under questionable circumstances. Trouble apparently found them in Silver City as well and it is said the Duke ended up in Leavenworth and the Duchess began taking in laundry.[15]

In 1956, Mattie Davis, a local real estate woman, her husband, James R. Davis, her brother, M. Fitzgerald, and sister-in-law, Anne T. Fitzgerald, bought the ranch for what is said to have been a "paltry sum." The

New Owners - Fred and Myra McCormick and their Land Rover

Davises and the Fitzgeralds assumed ownership of a set of buildings long without proper maintenance and certainly without the environment to attract visitors. During the next few years, there was a rumor that the town of Silver City was considering buying the ranch to use as a country club. There was also speculation that the charming ranch built by Walter and Juanita Langer in 1928, might be torn down and a golf clubhouse erected.[16] But in 1959, Myra B. and Frederick McCormick of Albuquerque laid those rumors to rest when they purchased the Bear Mountain Ranch from the Davises and Fitzgeralds and began what would be the longest and most successful tenure of ownership in its history. In what became her trademark—candid and sometimes abrasive statements—Myra McCormick likened realtor Davis to a spider, waiting three years for flies to come along to buy the ranch. "We were the flies," she said. "We took possession on June 1, 1959."[17]

CHAPTER IV ENDNOTES

1. Harry G. Allen Jr., brochure, p. 5 (author's library).

2. Harry G. Allen Jr., passim.

3. *Silver City Daily Press*, 1938.

4. *Silver City Daily Press*.

5. *Silver City Daily Press*.

6. *The Silver City Enterprise*, 16 February 1950.

7. *The Silver City Enterprise*.

8. *The Silver City Enterprise*.

9. *The Silver City Enterprise*.

10. G.R. Kinsinger, brochure, n.d. (author's library).

11. Kinsinger brochure.

12. McCormick, iv.

13. *The Silver City Enterprise*, 11 March, 1954.

14. *The Silver City Enterprise*.

15. McCormick, p. iv.

16. McCormick. p. v.

17. McCormick, p. v.

CHAPTER V

The McCormick Years: Hospitality and Bird Watching

When Myra McCormick died in 1999, she left Bear Mountain Ranch to the New Mexico Nature Conservancy with the stipulation that they continue to operate it as a haven for bird lovers and conservationists and with great respect for nature and the environment. The Conservancy has endeavored to do just that. But for 40 years it was Myra McCormick who reigned supreme as the mistress of one of the most unique and esoteric tourist lodges in the United States.

Bear Mountain Ranch became Myra's domain, a cozy inn with an exquisite outdoor laboratory for the study of nature and birds. When Myra and Fred bought the place in 1959, they had been looking for an opportunity that would take them out of a large city (Albuquerque), and provide for them a change of pace. Fred had grown up on a ranch in the Four Corners area (New Mexico, Arizona, Colorado and Utah) and

Myra McCormick serving meals at the Ranch.

Myra's family had operated a four-acre truck farm in Vineland, New Jersey. Myra had commuted from Vineland to Drexel University in Philadelphia and earned a bachelor of science degree in commercial education and secretarial studies. Over the years the couple had lived in Chicago, Los Angeles, the Philippines, Okinawa, Indiana, Michigan and Wisconsin, but once settled in at the Bear Mountain Ranch, they would never leave.[1]

Before buying Bear Mountain Ranch, they had looked at other hostelries, but decided upon this one because they thought even if business

Dining room at Bear Mountain Ranch during McCormick years.

was slow they could keep it open by housing college students. "All too soon," Myra said, "I realized the fallacy of that thinking, as many of the students at Western New Mexico University live at home."[2]

Old mining town building the McCormick's moved to the Ranch – now used as a volunteer's cabin.

When they took possession of the ranch, the buildings were in very bad condition due to a lack of maintanence for well over thirty years. Fred spent the early years working full-time at the ranch to get it back in shape. Remodeling and additions to the original buildings were necessary. In fact, work to improve the ranch never stopped. Under the McCormicks' ownership, one of the two cottages originally built as a garage became a separate little casita they called the Wren's Nest. Coyote Corner, a two-room cabin moved by the McCormicks in 1961 from the nearby mining town of Fiero,[3] is now used for a volunteer's quarters.

The McCormicks did their own marketing as well. In an early sepia-colored publicity brochure featuring Myra and Fred on the back cover, they invited guests to "Escape the heat in summer—Get away from the noise and bustle of city life—Vacation in a National forest four miles off U.S. 260 highway traffic noises…"[4] The brochure promoted activities like panning for gold, fishing deep in the heart of the Gila Wilderness "where few fishermen ever go," hunting in season, and a chance to see an open pit copper mine in operation.[5] It all paid off, because once they were up and going, the McCormicks began to make a name for the ranch.

The brochure, most likely used in the 1960s or '70s, listed rates as "$4.00 and up, with special family packages available."[6] Another flyer dated 1993, and listing the ranch as Bear Mountain Guest Ranch, showed bed and breakfast rates at $40 -$141 depending on which rooms were available and how many occupants were registered.[7] Such an increase was certainly a product of the times.

But, as with the Langers, misfortune befell Myra and Fred McCormick. Fred died unexpectedly in 1978 and Myra was left alone to run

Myra McCormick's personal brand.

People Birdwatching at the Ranch

the ranch, which she did for the next 20 years. She was not only the sole proprietor and manager, but she became well known all over the United States for the nature and bird-watching programs offered at the lodge. Harry Benjamin, a Silver City artist and friend of Myra McCormick's, remembers her interest in birds. "Myra was very involved in Audubon and that is how I met her…and she stayed involved up until her death."[8] Mr. Benjamin also remembered Myra as a serious conservationist and recalled the time she drove all the way to Oklahoma to appear before a national parks hearing regarding laws governing our national forests, "Myra was an environmental activist and she hated complacency when it came to taking care of our natural resources…she took very good care of the land while she had it. She ran her place as an educational place for people to come…She wasn't just there to entertain people…even up to making sure that no one ever threw away a paper napkin!"[9]

Throughout the years of Myra's reign as mistress of Bear Mountain Ranch, she offered much more than lodging and meals. There were workshops on bird watching, wild plant identification and archaeology. Visitors could also enjoy ghost town tours, trips to the Gila Cliff Dwellings National Monument and archaeology workshops that included visits to a Mimbres Classic Field House on her property, where 8,000 years earlier native people had lived.[10] An Old West environment was always present at Bear Mountain Ranch and Myra was especially proud to have

Myra and Border Collie "Sport" with ranch guests

Myra leading a group of guests to the Gila Cliff Dwellings

Myra and Guests at Dinner.

Myra and Friend

secured her own cattle brand.

A self-taught bird enthusiast, Myra Mc-Cormick often consulted with noted ornithologist Dr. Dale Zimmerman of Western New Mexico University regarding conservation issues, plant and bird identification, bird feeder locations, and the building of bird blinds for photography. Even though Myra herself conducted most field trips and bird-watching hikes, she often asked Dr. Zimmerman and other specialists to give talks at the lodge on birds, plants and butterflies. Myra was also instrumental in establishing the Southwestern New Mexico Audubon Society in 1968 and was an active member for more than two decades.[11]

Bear Mountain Ranch Recipes

by **MYRA McCORMICK**

Through the years, Myra also worked on a bird and plant inventory of the three ranges of desert mountains in southern New Mexico: Tres Hermanas, the Floridas and the Cooke's Range. In addition, she catalogued 100 species of birds in the area around the ranch.[12]

Besides conducting field trips and hikes, Myra handled the entire operation of the ranch with only a small support staff. Dr. Zimmerman remembered her as a very physical person, a "disciplined hiker" and a hard worker.[13] Because of the enormous responsibility of running the ranch almost single-handedly, Myra had little time for anything else. When Ruth Armstrong, a prolific freelance writer from Corrales,

Myra's dog "Tawny."

Ranch Cats

49

New Mexico, interviewed her in 1979 for an article in *Bird Watcher's Digest*, Myra told her that she rarely even had time to watch television. To prove her point, she relayed a story about famed movie star Steve McQueen and a party of six having come to the ranch one night without reservations. Myra welcomed them all, prepared dinner and settled them in rooms—never once recognizing McQueen. When another guest mentioned to her that Steve McQueen was there, Myra responded, "Steve who?"[14]

Myra McCormick may have also been before her time in promoting healthy food in the dining room. In a cookbook she wrote in 1989, she lists helpful hints for the kitchen which include suggestions for cooking

Myra McCormick – True Grit

health-conscious meals that any dietician would love. A few of her ideas that health food advocates promote today included reducing sugar and salt by half in all recipes; substituting non-fat powdered milk for milk, cream or half and half; and figuring serving sizes by weight.[15] Stories abound about her frugality in the kitchen and in all the ways she ran the ranch.

A former employee of Bear Mountain Ranch remembered that Myra ran a tight ship: "Myra was a stickler when it was time to clean the lodge. She wanted a homey environment, yet her rules were to be followed."[16] She also recalled that Myra would issue one towel and one wash cloth to each guest and that was it for their stay. Myra always insisted that guests come immediately for dinner when she rang a bell. Furthermore, she wanted them to be back at the lodge by a certain time each evening.[17]

It is obvious she ran the ranch with a tight grip, was frugal to a fault and quite conservative. Nonetheless, former guests often sent photographs of their stay at Bear Mountain Ranch, some containing notes to Myra suggesting they had a great time.

Guests from all over the world came to Bear Mountain Ranch— nature lovers, the environmentally sensitive, and those who came just for solitude. A guest book dated 1995-96, only three years before her death, listed visitors from France, England, Greece, Australia, Canada, Japan, Germany, Italy and Switzerland. Visitors came from hundreds of cities and towns across the United States as well and many were regulars from neighboring states. Entries in the same guest book for the month of May 1996, counting only one guest per line, suggests almost 100 percent occupancy with an average of five rooms occupied per day.[18]

Critters in the wild were Myra's greatest interest, but she loved domestic animals as well. Photos of the ranch during her tenure almost always include a dog or cat in her arms or within a short distance. A 1978 photo shows a snoozing St. Bernard by the name of Tawny and a caption notes that the dog is "the official greeter, loves all the guests." Another photo shows Myra posing with guests, along with a border collie named Sport, while others include dogs of questionable parentage. In almost all of her outdoor photos, a cat can be seen doing what cats do best—basking in the sunshine.

In addition to running every aspect of the ranch's operation, Myra worked hard to promote tourism in Silver City and pressured the local Chamber of Commerce to build a visitors' center. She also spearheaded a committee of local business people to sponsor a 10-day Silver City Discovery celebration. For a fee, visitors could tour Victorian homes, attend melodramas, shop at arts and crafts exhibits, or take a walking tour of historic neighborhoods, stopping at bird-watching stations along the way. The goal was to raise money for a permanent tourist information center. [19] (Silver City now has a fine Chamber of Commerce office and visitor center complex at 201 Hudson Avenue.)

Myra McCormick was a colorful character who left her mark on Silver City and the natural world around her. She continued to operate the ranch until illness forced her retirement, but had already made arrangements for it to be donated to the New Mexico Nature Conservancy upon her death. What a fitting gift to an agency that is dedicated to the preservation and study of wild life and the conservation of natural resources. Myra McCormick's gift to the world is one that will live on forever through the Conservancy. Her legacy and that of the Conservancy—the conservation of nature—are no doubt more vital to our planet's existence than ever before.

Myra McCormick and Juanita Franks were probably not unlike pioneer women who chose to spend their lives in the West. Both possessed determination, perseverance and grit—as well as a deep love of nature. Moreover, they fall into a special category—unforgettable women of the 20th century.

Bear Mountain Ranch during McCormick Years.

Bear Mountain Ranch at Christmas.

Myra McCormick – Proprietress of Bear Mountain Ranch for 40 years.

CHAPTER V ENDNOTES

1. McCormick, p. v.

2. McCormick, p. v.

3. McCormick, p. v.

4. Fred and Myra McCormick Bear Mountain Ranch brochure, n.d. (author's library).

5. McCormick Bear Mountain Ranch brochure.

6. McCormick Bear Mountain Ranch brochure.

7. Bear Mountain Guest Ranch Brochure. (author's library).

8. Interview with Harry Benjamin, Silver City, New Mexico, by Donna Eichstaedt, 25 August 2007.

9. Eichstaedt interview with Harry Benjamin.

10. McCormick, p. vi.

11. Interview with Dr. Dale Zimmerman, Silver City, New Mexico, by Donna Eichstaedt, 26 November 2007.

12. Ruth W. Armstrong. "She Combines Business with Birding." *Bird Watcher's Digest*, November/December 1979, p. 30.

13. Eichstaedt interview with Dr. Dale Zimmerman.

14. Ruth W. Armstrong, p. 28.

15. McCormick, p.ii.

16. Joanne Cross, Silver City, New Mexico. Interview by Donna Eichstaedt, 2 November 2008.

17. Maura Gonsior, Silver City, New Mexico. Interview by Donna Eichstaedt, 15 January 2008.

18. Bear Mountain Ranch Guest Book (author's library).

19. Eichstaedt interview with Harry Benjamin.

EPILOGUE

The New Mexico Nature Conservancy's Bear Mountain Lodge: "Comfort and Conservation"

A headline on page one of the *Silver City Daily Press*, on February 26, 2000, told readers that Myra McCormick had bequeathed the Bear Mountain Ranch to the Nature Conservancy of New Mexico. That gift would mean the end of 72 years of private family ownership and the beginning of a new era in the ranch's history.

The Nature Conservancy is a private, non-profit, international conservation organization that has protected more than 11 million acres of land in the United States and 60 million acres internationally. Its presence in New Mexico began in 1973, and since then, more than 1.1 million acres across the state have been preserved. Its mission is to "preserve plants, animals and natural communities that represent the diversity of life on Earth by protecting the lands and waters they need to survive."[1] It was a perfect match—the Bear Mountain Ranch and the Nature Conservancy.

Remodeling and enlarging the ranch became a priority to better serve as a premier eco-tourism destination. Project Director Bob Findling announced a name change from Bear Mountain Ranch to Bear Mountain Lodge and promised a "comfortable B & B experience while at the same time educating guests about nature and protection of the environment."[2] The Conservancy added trails to connect to the Gila National Forest, and upon taking ownership, purchased additional land, increasing the property size from 160 acres to 178.[3]

Silver City contractor Rich Bigelow began renovating and remodeling the lodge in 2000 in a project that took about nine months to complete. He noted that the original building's exterior walls were constructed with clay-fired brick, common during that time period and used in commercial buildings and prisons. The bricks, also known as prison brick, have no insulation value, thus the renovation required additional framing and insulation. The original great room, staircase and upstairs landing and hall remained the same, though the vigas and beams were sandblasted and sealed. Both great room fireplaces were repaired, with new stucco horse sculptures added. The remodeling and expansion brought the total number of bedrooms in the main lodge to six, all with private bathrooms.

Renovation of the Bear Mountain Lodge

One of the two guest rooms on the main floor is the Gila and the other, the Mimbres, is handicapped accessible. Also added to the main floor is an additional bathroom, a library with reference materials, and expanded kitchen and storage areas.

Newly remodeled Lodge Great Room

The east and west wings were extended, the dining room redecorated, and porches added. At the south end of the dining room, which was once a porch where the boys at Walter and Juanita's Rocky Mountain Ranch school slept year round, is a cozy reading area, book-shelves and a computer for guest use.

The four bedrooms on the second floor, now named O'Keefe, Leopold, Emory and Cabeza de Vaca guest rooms, were remodeled and feature large balconies. The front porch was also transformed, adding an arch--typical of the 1920s and '30s.

A remodeled bedroom at the Lodge

The building behind the main lodge, Myra's Retreat, named after Myra McCor-mick, houses four guest rooms (Hummingbird, Warbler, Bluebird and Roadrunner), and features a new front porch and a central living/reading room. Across from Myra's

Added porch

Myra's Retreat behind main lodge

One of the many trails at the Lodge

Retreat is the Wren's Nest, a newly remodeled cottage featuring a kitchen for extended stays. Just north of Myra's Retreat is Coyote Cabin, where a naturalist's helper lives. These people are chosen from a pool of applicants from all over the United States and volunteer for three months at a time.[5]

A recent Bear Mountain Lodge brochure invites guests to enjoy an "exquisitely renovated 1920s guest house that offers considerable charm, comfortable suites, private baths and delicious home cooked meals."[6] To enhance the ambience of the lodge, the furniture is handcrafted in mission style, with upholstery in soft earth tones.

There are no provisions for children under 10 or pets, but for a $15 per night fee, guests can bring a horse. Bear Mountain Lodge is a smoke-free inn and accommodations come with breakfast. Lunch and dinner are available with prior notice, and for long day excursions, sack lunches can be ordered. The lodge also features workshops, which for 2007 included Mimbreño art, photography, Native American lore, history, astronomy and archaeology.[7]

Six trails spring from the lodge in almost every direction, with one even crossing the Continental Divide. They are well-marked and relatively easy hikes. Wildlife is abundant and there are frequent sightings of mule deer, wild turkey, or some of the 300 different species of birds who call the area their home. Common to the area are Mexican jays, the mountain chickadee and a variety of hawks[8]. Each morning and evening, a herd of mule deer entertains guests by drinking from a small pond and man-made creek behind the lodge. They enjoy stealing birdseed from feeders on the property and allow guests to photograph and admire them. A full-time naturalist is in residence at the lodge, and other scholars are called in to lead hikes and teach special topics. The lodge is also available for weddings, family reunions and conferences.[9]

Juanita Franks and Walter Langer created a precious gift of nature when they built the Bear Mountain Lodge in 1928 and Myra McCormick ensured the continuation of that gift when she left it in her will to the Nature Conservancy. And now, it can also be said that the New Mexico Nature Conservancy is continuing that tradition—a gift, as the saying goes, that just keeps on giving.

A regular visitor at the Lodge

An unregistered guest at the Lodge

View from one of the trails above the Lodge

Entrance to the Lodge

EPILOGUE ENDNOTES

1. New Mexico Nature Conservancy brochure.

2. *Silver City Daily Press*, 26 February 2000.

3. Eichstaedt interview with Maura Gonsior.

4. Richard Bigelow, Silver City, New Mexico. Interview by Donna Eichstaedt, 11, October 2007.

5. Eichstaedt interview with Maura Gonsior.

6. Bear Mountain Lodge brochure.

7. Bear Mountain Lodge brochure.

8. Bear Mountain Lodge brochure.

9. Bear Mountain Lodge brochure.

The Mission of the Nature Conservancy is to preserve plants, animals and natural communities that represent the diversity of life on Earth by protecting the lands and waters they need to survive.

Juanita Franks' Advice for Living to 103 Years Old

Stay away from doctors and lawyers!!!

Look for the good in everyone.

Take care of yourself first or you're no good to anyone else!

Take care of your family first. Charity begins at home.

Own a pet or 2 or 3 or if you're Juanita own 20 (2 dogs, 3 frogs, 13 chickens and 2 turkeys).

Laugh a lot. There is humor in every situation.

Eat a well balanced diet with lots of fruits and veggies. Make sure you drink plenty of water.

Be nice to everyone. It doesn't cost you a thing.

Don't feel sorry for yourself it isn't hard to find someone in worse shape than you. Dust yourself off and get back in there and buck.

Enjoy life. Tell those you care about how much you love them and get lots of hugs.

Life is too short. Don't sweat the small stuff and if no one is dying or having a life changing event it's small stuff.

BIBLIOGRAPHY

Books

Langer, William. *The Illustrious Langers: In and Out of the Ivory Tower*. New York: Neale Watson Academic Publishing Company, 1977.

Langer, Walter C. *Psychology and Human Living*. New York: D. Appleton –Century Col., 1943.

_____ *The Mind of Adolf Hitler: The Secret Wartime Report*. New York: Basic Books, Inc., 1972.

McCormick, Myra. *Bear Mountain Ranch Recipes*. Tucson: Sahuaro Press, 1989.

Articles

Armstrong, Ruth W. "She Combines Business with Birding." *Bird Watcher's Digest*, November/December 1979, 28-30.

Coan, Charles. "History of New Mexico." *The American Historical Review*, (April 1927): 366-67.

Langer, Walter C. and Sanford Gifford. "An American Analyst in Vienna during the Anschluss: 1936-1938." *Journal of the History of the Behavioral Sciences* XIV (January 1978): 37-54.

Lynn, Sandra D. "Conservancy Lands Retreat." *New Mexico Magazine*, April 1997, 17, 19.

Newspapers

"Bear Mountain Ranch: Silver City, New Mexico." *Silver City Daily Press*,1938 Progress Edition, p. 5.

"Bear Mountain Lodge Is Opened as Nursing Convalescent Home." *Silver City Enterprise*, 16 February 1950.

"Bear Mountain Lodge Newest Dude Ranch in Vast Recreation Area." *Silver City Enterprise*, 17 June 1932.

"Formal Opening of the Bear Mountain Country Club." *The Silver City Enterprise*, 22 July 1932, n.p.

"Group Takes Over Bear Mountain Ranch." *Silver City Daily Press*, 26 February 2000, p. 1.

"Inez Horton Sells Bear Mountain Ranch." *Silver City Enterprise*, 13 June 1946, p. 3.

"Juanita Franks: 'So Much to Tell You.'" *Silver City Sun News*, 1 November 1999, A-3.

"Langer Home North of City Converted to Country Club." *Silver City Independent*, ll June 1932, p. 6.

"Official Allied Profile of Hitler Declassified." *New York Times*, 10 September 1972,n.p.

"Seven Escape As Fire Razes Boys' School in Auburndale." *The Boston Globe*, 9 December 1931, p. l.

"Silver City Woman Will be Back in the Saddle Again on her 100th Birthday." *Silver City Daily Press*, 13 January 2003, n.p.

"Time to Get Away: Head for the Hills." *Las Cruces Sun News*, 14 October, 2001, C-1.

"Zaagmans Buy Bear Mountain Ranch." *Silver City Enterprise*, 11 March, 1954, n.p.

Proceedings

Gifford, Sanford, M.D. "The Rediscovery of Walter Langer, 1899-1981." *Colloquium on the History of Psychiatry*, Countway Medical Library, Harvard Medical School, Cambridge, Massachusetts.: 4 November 1999, Cambridge, Massachusetts (printed).

Government Documents

New Mexico, Grant County, Deed Record Books, 61, 85, 130.

U.S. Office of Strategic Services. "Psychological Analysis of Adolf Hitler: His Life And Legends." http://www.lawschool.cornell.edu/library/donovan/hitler/" http://www.lawschool.cornell.edu/library donovan/hitler/

Unpublished Materials

Allen, Harry G., Jr. "Bear Mountain Ranch, Silver City, New Mexico." Brochure, 1937, (author's library).

Boston Psychoanalytic Society and Institute Archives. Boston, Massachusetts, Walter Langer Papers, 1935-2001, Ms. N-007.

_____Boston, Massachusetts, Walter Langer Papers, 1972-1981, Ms. N-007.

Kinsinger, G.R. "Bear Mountain Ranch." Brochure, n.d. (author's library)

McCormick, Fred. "Bear Mountain Ranch, Silver City, New Mexico." Brochure, n.d. (author's library).

Langer, Walter C. "The Rocky Mountain Ranch School." Silver City, New Mexico, Brochure, n.d. (author's library).

_____. "A Mental Hygiene School for Boys." Silver City, New Mexico, Booklet, 1928. (author's library).

The Nature Conservancy of New Mexico Brochure, "Bear Mountain Lodge," n.d.

Silver City, New Mexico. "History of Bear Mountain Lodge," typed manuscript, no author, n.d.

Silver City, New Mexico Chamber of Commerce Brochure, "Bear Mountain Ranch." 2007.

Silver City, New Mexico. "Bear Mountain Guest Ranch," Brochure, n.d. (author's Library).

Interviews

Benjamin, Harry. Silver City, New Mexico. Interview, 25 August 2007.

Bigelow, Richard. Silver City, New Mexico. Interview, 11 October 2007.

Cross, Joanne Woodward. Silver City, New Mexico. Interview, 2 November 2007.

Franks, Juanita. Silver City, New Mexico. Interview, 1 August 2002.

_____. Boston Psychoanalytic Institute, Boston, Massachusetts Interview by Dr. Sanford Gifford, M.D., 22 May, 1999. (Transcript)

Gonsior, Maura. Silver City, New Mexico. Interview, 15 January 2008.

Rowse, Linda. Silver City, New Mexico. Interview, 25 August 2007.

Sullivan, Terry. The Nature Conservancy of New Mexico. Interview, 2 December 2003.

Zimmerman, Dr. Dale. Silver City, New Mexico. Interview, 26 November 2007.

World Wide Web Sites

Boston Psychoanalytic Society and Institute Archives Website, 17 July 2007. http://www.bostonpsychoanalytic.org/library

INDEX

Allen, Harry, Jr., 22,23,39.
Annisquam, Massachusetts, 36.
Anschluss, 29.
Armstrong, Ruth, 49.
Atlantic City, New Jersey, 21.
Auburndale, Massachusetts, 18, 19.

Battle of the Bulge, 27.
Bear Mountain, 1.
Bear Mountain Lodge, 2,16, 21, 22, 27, 57, 58, 59, 61, 62, 63.
Bear Mountain Ranch, 232, 29, 40, 41, 45, 47, 49, 51, 53, 54, 57.
Bear Mountain Rest Home, 40.
Benjamin, Harry, 47.
Bigelow, Rich, 57.
Border Patrol, 29.
Boston, Massachusetts, 11, 18, 20, 21, 31, 34, 36.
Boston Psychoanalytic Society & Institute, 19.

Castle Inn Hotel, 19.
Cherbourg, France, 31.
Columbia Teachers' College, 22.

Davis, Mattie, 42.
Davis, James, 42.
D'Autry, Duke and Duchess, 42.
D-Day, 27.
Denver School of Social Work, 22.
Drexel University, 45.
Dye, Lillie and Samps, 1.

Eisenhower, General Dwight D., 27.

Findling, Bob, 57.
Fitzgerald, M. and Anne, 42.
Fort Bayard Veterans' Hospital, 27.

Franks, Alvin, 2, 6, 12,15,16, 20, 21.
Franks, Lolabelle, 2.
Franks, Juanita, 1, 2, 5, 6, 7, 10, 11, 17, 19, 20, 21, 22, 27, 28, 29, 42, 52, 59, 61. 68.
Franks, Maggie Flurry, 1, 2, 5, 7.
Franks, Randolph, 2.
Franks, Shirley, 1, 2.
Franks, William C., 1, 2, 5.
Frankfurter, Felix, 32.
Freud, Sigmund, 6, 17, 22, 25, 27, 29, 30, 32, 34, 35.
Freud, Anna, 29, 30, 32, 33.
Frymire, Carl, 22.

Garrett, Pat, 1.
Geer, Will, 41.
Gestapo, 31, 32.
Gifford, Sanford M.D., 19.
Gila Cliff Dwellings, 40, 47, 48.
Gila National Forest, 1, 17, 21, 40, 47, 48.
Grinzing, Austria, 29.

Harvard University, 2, 5, 18, 20, 22 30.
Hitler, Adolf, 21, 22, 28, 30, 34, 36.
Horton, Mr. and Mrs., 39, 40, 41.

Ivanhoe, New Mexico, 17.

Kinsinger, Anna and George, 40, 41.

Langer, Leonard, 20.
Langer, Rudolph, 17.
Langer, Walter, 2, 5, 6, 7, 9, 10, 11, 17, 19, 20, 21, 22, 29, 30, 31, 32, 33, 34, 42, 59, 61.
Langer, William, 17, 49.
Langer School for Boys, 19.

McCormick, Fred, 41,42,45,46, 47,48,49.
McCormick, Myra, 3, 41, 42, 45, 46, 47, 48, 49, 50, 51, 52, 53, 54, 57.

McQueen, Steve, 50.

New Deal, 22.
New Mexico Nature Conservancy, 2, 36, 43, 49, 57, 61, 67.
New Mexico Territory, 1.

Office of Strategic Services (OSS), 34.

Pete Paine, 5,6,7.
Peck, Dr. Martin, 10.
Pinos Altos, New Mexico, 17, 40.

Pulsifer Estate, 19.

Queen Mary, 31.

Red Cross, 29.
Rindge Technical School, 18.
Rocky Mountain Ranch School, 7, 8, 10, 12.
Franklin Delano Roosevelt, 22,32.
Rowse, Linda, 29.

Sarasota, Florida, 28.
Silver City Chamber of Commerce, 52.

Townsend, Mrs. Charles, 40.

V-1 and V-2 Rockets, 27.
Vienna, Austria, 29, 30, 31, 32, 33, 34.
Vineland, New Jersey, 45.
Vienna Psychoanalytic Institute, 17, 29, 31.

Western New Mexico University, 17, 46, 49.
Winkle, J.R., 41.
Winsor, Frederick, 5, 7.
Woodward, Clarence, 7.
Woodward, Walter, 7.
World War I. 6, 12, 18.

World War II., 15, 34.